YOUR KNOWLEDGE HAS VALUE

Eric Vanderburg

Implementing a Best Practice Risk Assessment Methodology

GRIN Publishing

Bibliographic information published by the German National Library:

The German National Library lists this publication in the National Bibliography; detailed bibliographic data are available on the Internet at http://dnb.dnb.de .

Imprint:

Copyright © 2013 GRIN Verlag GmbH
Print and binding: Books on Demand GmbH, Norderstedt Germany
ISBN: 978-3-656-82045-1

This book at GRIN:

http://www.grin.com/en/e-book/282608/implementing-a-best-practice-risk-assess-ment-methodology

GRIN - Your knowledge has value

Since its foundation in 1998, GRIN has specialized in publishing academic texts by students, college teachers and other academics as e-book and printed book. The website www.grin.com is an ideal platform for presenting term papers, final papers, scientific essays, dissertations and specialist books.

Visit us on the internet:

http://www.grin.com/

http://www.facebook.com/grincom

http://www.twitter.com/grin_com

Implementing a Best Practice Risk

Assessment Methodology

Eric Vanderburg

Table of Contents

I. Overview

Implementing a best practice risk assessment involves a risk assessment methodology describing how to perform Information Technology risk assessments. Risk assessments play a critical role in the development and implementation of effective information security programs and help address a range of security related issues from advanced persistent threats to supply chain concerns.

The results of risk assessments are used to develop specific courses of action that can provide effective response measures to the identified risks as part of a broad-based risk management process.

The guidance provided here uses the key risk factors of threats, vulnerabilities, impact to missions and business operations, and the likelihood of threat exploitation of weaknesses in information systems and environments of operation, to help senior leaders and executives understand and assess the current information security risks to information technology infrastructure. The risk assessment guidance has been designed to have maximum flexibility so the process can meet the needs of many types of companies.

The risk assessment guidance is consistent with the process for managing information security risk described in NIST Special Publication 800-39 that includes framing risk, assessing risk, responding to risk and monitoring risk over time risks to the organization's operations (including missions, functions, image, and reputation), the organization's critical assets, individuals who are part of the organization or who the organization serves, other entities involved in partnerships or collaborative efforts with the organization, and the Nation at large (including critical infrastructure). The guidance also supports a three-tier (Tier 1 - organization level, Tier 2 - mission/business process level, and Tier 3 - information system level) enterprise-wide risk management approach which focuses on the organization's governance structures; the organization's core missions/business functions, mission/business processes, and enterprise architecture; and the organization's information systems that are essential for mission/business success. Copies of Special Publication 800-30, Revision 1, can be obtained from the NIST Computer Security Division web site at: http://csrc.nist.gov/publications.

II. Scope

This risk assessment methodology identifies how organizations can classify the inherent risks that it may face. The document further gives insights on how risk assessment helps in company planning, improves risk management processes and outlines the steps involved in risk assessment, including communicating risk assessment results to everyone involved and maintaining the standards of risk assessment

III. About the author

Eric Vanderburg is a graduate from Kent State University with a Bachelor of Science in Technology and a Masters of Business Administration with a concentration in Information Systems. During and after his education he worked as a consultant specializing in the development and maintenance of information management and network security systems for businesses, law firms, and government agencies. He has worked in education as a professor of computer networking at Remington College where he taught courses on information security, database systems, and computer networking and as a professor of computer information systems at Lorain County Community College.

Eric Vanderburg has been invited to speak at many organizations and campuses on technology and information security. Vanderburg was awarded an honorary Ph.D from Vatterott College in 2010 for his work in raising awareness of information security and promoting security and technology education. He holds over 30 vendor certifications including: Certified Information Systems Security Professional (CISSP), Holistic Information Security Practitioner (HISP), Certified Wireless Security Professional (CWSP), Hitachi Data Systems Certified Professional (HDSCP), and many certifications from Microsoft and Cisco.

1 Introduction

It is highly important for an organization to understand the key risks involved in doing business in order to avoid compromising integrity and confidentiality of the data present on systems or handled by the company. With many threats introduced every day, I recommend that the person filling the risk management role at a company should be on top of the threats and vulnerabilities and document risks. The latter is accomplished primarily through risk assessments.

Risk assessments inform the decision makers and other stakeholders about the possible threats on business processes. It also describes when the risk is possible to strike the functioning of the business and the methods to overcome the same. Companies should conduct and adapt risk assessment at levels ranging from organizational level to business process level to information system level. Once risk assessment is ready, I recommend that a company implement risk management methodologies that include designing, implementing, testing and monitoring security guidelines. The most important audience for risk assessment framework is people who are responsible for risk management, security analysts, developers, designers and managers.

2 Risk management

Risk management involves four important steps. They are:

1. Framing risk
2. Assessing risk
3. Responding to risk
4. Monitoring risk

2.1 Framing risk

The first step is the most important step since it defines what the risk is and how the risk may impact the organization's activities. When risks are framed, it becomes easier for an organization to assess the risk and monitor the same to avoid unwanted problems. Once framing risks is completed, it is necessary to assess the impact of risk on the existing applications and organizational data. Risk assessment process provides results that help prevent business failures. Assessing the risk will also help in identifying when the risk might occur and possible repercussions of the risk. The third step is also an important one as it determines what actions an organization takes to overcome the risks. It also includes the preventive measures that can be taken in order to prevent the risk from damaging the system. Possible solutions to overcome risks are to identify alternative solutions for the requirement, identify methods to overcome risk and implementing security practices. When all of these steps are completed, the fourth step – monitoring risk - plays a vital role since it determines when the risk will strike again. This will also determine the effectiveness of actions taken to prevent and overcome risks.

2.2 Assessing risk

With four steps listed above, let's concentrate on the second one, risk assessment, as it provides necessary precautions for organization to tackle risks. Once risks are assessed, they need to be communicated to the entire team. This can prevent risks from being introduced at level of ownership.

Risks are likely to occur in of the following phases of software process including development of new software service, interconnecting various networking and information systems, designing and implementing security solutions along with maintenance of security solutions, integrity and authorization processes. The most important point to remember with respect to risk assessment is the time period for which it is valid. As said above, the advent of new technologies have also resulted in development of new threats. Hence, a risk assessment valid today might not be valid tomorrow. This makes it a time bound process and needs to be repeated at shorter duration of time.

Before delving deep into risk assessment, let's understand the basic terminologies associated with risk and its impacts on organization. Risk is defined as the measure of threat that an organization possess in terms of integrity and confidentiality of the business processes. I recommend that risks should be analyzed along with the extent of threat it poses and the likelihood of its occurrence. When these data are analyzed and documented in proper standards, it is called risk assessment. A risk assessment framework should include four important components:

1. Risk assessment process
2. Risk model
3. Assessment approach
4. Analysis approach

2.2.1 Risk assessment process

Risk assessment is a process by which the risk and its associated components are analyzed. Risk model defines the various factors associated with the risk and the assessment approach defines the various values that are used during the analysis of risk. Analysis approach provides user with information related to coverage of various processes under risk management. The four components mentioned above will determine the risk assessment methodology of organization. The other factors that help in determining this methodology are the time frame available for the business to implement the solution, the complexity of the risk and the impact of risk on existing processes, the modules that are affected and the sensitivity of the information that will be compromised. Hence, it is the responsibility of the information technology analysts to identify the proper risk analysis approach, assessment approach to determine risk management methodology.

2.2.2 Risk models

Risk models are the various risk factors that will determine the relationships of the risk factors and their impact on the functioning of the business. The risk factors are also used in communicating the risk details to other members at various levels of organization. The risk model consists of:

1. Threat
2. Vulnerability
3. Likelihood

4. Impact
5. Aggregation
6. Uncertainty

2.1.2.1 Threat

It is important to understand the various sources of threats so as to formulate risk assessments. The various sources of threat include physical attacks, source code error, structural failures etc.

2.1.2.2 Vulnerability

Risk is closely associated with vulnerability as the latter is defined as a weakness in applications that will give rise to risk in security controls and procedures. Vulnerabilities occur when the security protocols have not been applied completely or when they are applied only partially. Also, there is the possibility for a new vulnerability to be introduced when an application is in use for a longer period of time.

Apart from causing damage to organization data, vulnerabilities can also cause damage to organizational governance and external relationships. Vulnerabilities when combined with threats results in risks. The threat scenarios help an organization to analyze the various areas of threats so that preventive action can be carried out when needed. There are some vulnerability that are exploited only when some other vulnerabilities occur and this is where a threat scenario comes into action as it presents information on the origin of the threat.

2.1.2.3 Likelihood

Likelihood is the possibility of the occurrence of a risk factor, given the vulnerabilities and threats. The adversary threats can be measured using adversary intent, capability and targeting. When the threat is not adversarial, their likelihood can be measured using past evidences and other factors that will contribute to the threat. Some threats are also capable of repeating itself over a certain period of time and such threats are easily determined for likelihood.

There are three steps in determining the likelihood of a threat event. In the first step, organization will analyze the likelihood of events getting initiated followed by the likelihood of causing trouble to the assets and other valuable resources of organization. These steps are followed by the analysis of likelihood of combination of initiation and impact of threats. Since there are possibly large number of threats and vulnerabilities, it is difficult for the threat vulnerability pairing to take place.

2.1.2.4 Impact

Impact is defined as the extent to which risks and threats cause destruction to the integrity, credibility and confidentiality of the data present at various levels of the organization. It is necessary for the business process to analyze the impact of the threats and risks along with methods for communicating the same to the team members. These factors play a vital role in the risk model as it summarizes the entire process of initiating a threat source to causing organizational risk. A threat source is first identified along with the various characteristics such as intent and capability of the threat. The threat source initiates the threat event based on the likelihood analysis. The threat event possesses sequence of steps ranging from actions to scenarios that exploits the vulnerability present in the application. These scenarios cause adverse impact in organization causing risks that will damage the confidentiality and integrity of the data.

2.1.2.5 Aggregation

Aggregation is defined as combining various low-level risks to form a single high-level risk. This will help organization to manage the risk assessment techniques that will manage the information systems and processes. There are cases when the risk assessment at the initial stage will not be the same at later stage. Hence the impact of the risks on organization goes beyond the expected level forcing managers to take immediate action to minimize damage. When the defects have direct relationship with others, they will be aggregated.

2.1.2.6 Uncertainty

There is a level of uncertainty in the calculation of risk and this uncertainty is attributed to various factors. The most important of them are inability to completely predict the future when compared with the past and incorrect knowledge on the impacts of the threats. The other factors include unidentified threats and vulnerabilities along with incorrectly calculated dependencies. Uncertainty can also be caused due to incomplete knowledge of various risks that are associated with the information and security systems that are already employed within organization. When risk assessment is analyzed and is shared with the team, I recommend that the uncertainty due to the above reasons should also be communicated.

2.2.3 Risk assessment approaches

There are three major approaches for risk assessment. They include the quantitative approach, qualitative approach and hybrid approach. There are various factors that come into picture when of the above three approaches are selected by organization for their risk assessment. Every approach has its set of advantages and disadvantages and it depends on the organization's work culture and historical evidences in selecting the approach.

2.2.3.1 Quantitative

Quantitative risk assessment approach employs principles, rules and techniques which will assess risks in the form of numbers. Even though this method will help in cost benefit analysis of organization, the interpretation of results and numbers make it a tougher option for the managers. The head of organization may question the results of the assessments as the numbers are not expected to give valid justification for the research as the quantitative assessment tends to be assigned based on the assessor's perception and not a definitive number.

2.2.3.2 Qualitative

Qualitative assessments use methods and tools to produce results of risk assessments in the form of levels or severity. The common example of qualitative results is the use of levels such as low, medium, high and very high etc. The advantage of using such approach is its simplicity in communicating the risks to the product owners but the disadvantage lies in the fact that only fewer values can be used for declaring the results.

2.2.3.3 Hybrid

And this is where hybrid approach came into picture. It combines the power of both quantitative approach and qualitative approach by employing tools and techniques that will define the results of the approach in scales or bins. Scale may be the range of numbers from a minimum value to a maximum value. The benefits of both quantitative and qualitative approach can be reaped in with the use of hybrid assessments.

2.2.4   Risk analysis approaches

The risk assessment approaches depend on the risk assessment document and the level of details present in the document. There are three approaches for risk analysis and they are generally oriented in one of the following three ways:

1.   Threat oriented

2.   Asset oriented

3.   Vulnerability oriented

2.2.4.1 Threat oriented

In threat oriented approach, the threat events and scenarios are taken into consideration. Based on this, the threat sources are updated. The vulnerabilities are identified and the risk is analyzed based on the likelihood of the threat. Factors such as location, natural disasters, attackers and financial issues are examples of threats.

2.2.4.2 Asset oriented

In asset oriented approach, the impact of the threat on the business process analysis is used for the analysis. Scores ranging from 0-10 are used to rank the importance of each asset with 10 indicating the highest rank and therefore the most critical.

Asset oriented level	Description	Explanation
Low	Moderately serious	The risk will result in damage, requiring repairs, to an asset or resource.
Moderate	Very serious	The risk will result in major damage, requiring extensive repairs to assets or resources.
High	Catastrophic	The risk will result in the loss of major assets.

2.2.4.3 Vulnerability oriented

The vulnerability approach uses the presence of preconditions or vulnerabilities that are identified during threat analysis. Also the threat events that are expected to arrive due to the vulnerabilities in the system.

Even though the risk analysis approaches are different in papers, they produce the same result as the factors considered for the approaches are same. Sometimes, differences arise with the starting point of the assessment, causing changes in the results of the risk analysis. This will also result in missing out threats and risks. This brought the introduction of a new approach that combined the benefits of both threat oriented approach and asset oriented approach.

Apart from the analysis approaches mentioned above, a couple of other analysis techniques such as graph based analysis are introduced that will bring out the relationship between threat sources and events, events and vulnerabilities and events and impacts. The relationship between threat sources and threat events is that a single threat source may cause multiple threat events and a single threat event may be a result of multiple threat sources. In a similar way, a single threat event will expose multiple vulnerabilities and a single vulnerability will cause multiple threat events. Apart from this, there are some rigorous approaches as well that will analyze the risks.

I recommend that organization consider various factors in selecting the type of risk assessment approach and risk analysis approach. Sometimes, there will be differences within organization itself that one approach will be used in the early part of the software development life cycle and another approach will be used in the later part.

2.3 Responding to risk

The goal of the risk response is to reduce risk(s) to the lowest acceptable residual risk level. This includes prioritizing risks and implementing the treatment measures identified during the assessment. Organizations must apply one or more of the following measures:

Avoidance: Avoid the risk by eliminating it via alteration of business practice, applying technology, etc.

Mitigation: Reduce the level of risk and/or its impact to organization.

Transfer: Transfer the risk to another organization (e.g., vendor or business partner) via contractual agreement, or insurance policy.

Manage: Choose to accept and manage the risk.

2.4 Monitoring risk

Risks and their factors (asset value, impacts, threats, vulnerabilities, and likelihood) must be monitored and reviewed regularly to identify any changes. Monitoring of risk based information is necessary for organization to stay on top of all risks. Also, threat events and sources change now and then causing new threats and vulnerabilities. Monitoring the risk assessment will ensure that organizations are aware of new threat sources and the likelihood and risks of threats. Organizations should also be aware of new information systems, businesses processes and functions that will result in a likelihood of threats. The main objective of this process to make sure that all the processes behave as expected. Maintaining risk assessment includes monitoring both the risk factors and updating risk assessment document. Monitoring the risk factors will prevent further risks while updating risk document will keep all entities updated on latest risks and likelihood of threat events. The frequency of risk assessment updates is decided by organization based on various factors. One of the important factors in deciding the frequency of updating risk assessment is the severity of risk and impact of risk on business process and function. Also, organization needs to decide on what chapters in the risk assessment document need to be updated. There have been cases when the entire document needs to be updated because of changes in organization's policy. But most often, the document is updated only for new threats, vulnerabilities, risk factors, likelihood and impact of risks. The updates to the risk assessment document should also be communicated to all relevant parties within organization.

3 Preparing for the risk assessment

The first and foremost step of risk assessment process is the preparation for the assessment as you will want to set the requirements upfront for the process to be carried out without trouble. The results of the risk management process are used as inputs for deciding the context of the assessment. Answers to questions such as what is the purpose of the assessment, what is the scope of the assessment, what are the assumptions that are required for carrying out the assessment, what the various sources of input for the assessment etc., can be obtained at the end of this vital process.

3.1 Purpose

The first sub task of preparing for the assessment is to identify the purpose of carrying out the assessment. It is necessary to understand why risk assessment is necessary and how it will benefit organization. The supplemental guidance will provide information on the purpose of the risk assessment. Also, the techniques that can be employed for risk assessment are given in the guidance along with expected results. Risk assessments that are carried out at tier 3 will help in identifying authorization details used in the complete software development life cycle, reciprocity and risk management. The risk assessment at tier 2 will help organization understand the various types of risks and information on how to react when the risks occur. It will provide assumptions and predisposing conditions on how to prevent future threat attacks. Risk assessments at tier 1 will help organization understand the risk executive functions that serve as the input for risk assessment methodology. I recommend that these steps be carried out whenever a new threat or vulnerability is exploited in the cyber world. There can be two types of risk assessment based on the timeframe in which it is carried out. When a risk assessment is carried out in the initial stages of organization business processes, they are said to be initial assessment. The other type is the subsequent assessment to the initial assessment which is carried out to keep risk assessment up to date. An initial assessment will provide results such as the basic threats and vulnerabilities present in the system while the subsequent assessment will provide results similar to comparative analysis of various risks and threats.

3.2 Scope

The next sub task in preparing for risk assessment is identifying the scope of the assessment such as time frame available, technological factors and organizational requirements. The scope of the assessment will include results on what tiers should be affected as part of assessment along with what entities of the organization will have an impact. The scope will also provide the timeframe on how long the risk assessment will be valid and when it should be updated.

The organizational applicability section lists the details of which departments or stakeholders will be affected by the results of risk assessment.

There are three types of business processes:

Management processes, the processes that govern the operation of a system. Typical management processes include "corporate governance" and "strategic management".

Operational processes, processes that constitute the core business and create the primary value stream. Typical operational processes are purchasing, manufacturing, advertising and marketing, and sales.

Supporting processes, which support the core processes. Examples include accounting, recruitment, call center, technical support. When it comes to time frame up to which risk assessment stays valid, the risk assessment on tier 1 should be valid for a longer period of time as organization change their policies only after many years. But the risk assessment of tier 3 should be updated periodically as it is valid only up to next release of the software.

3.3 Assumptions

This step will enable the organization to set up assumptions and constraints for the risk assessment process. organization will desire to state the assumptions that are in place for the risk assessment process. The assumptions need to be documented so that the stakeholders can have access to it. When the assumptions are made public, the risk model that is used can be reciprocated as and when needed. Assumptions are identified in various stages and areas of organization including threat events and sources, vulnerabilities, impacts and risk analysis approaches. Apart from assumptions, it is also necessary to explicitly state constraints in various levels of risk assessment including resources needed for assessment, skills, operational conditions etc. Once the risk assessment is performed, the assumptions are compared with original values. Assumptions need not be calculated every time risk assessment is performed. Assumptions come in handy during initial assessments and when they are documented, they can be used for re-assessments. For threat sources, organization should determine which one of them will cause major impact. This information is made explicit so that future steps in risk assessment can use the assumptions. The same is followed for other threat events, vulnerabilities, predisposing conditions, likelihood and impacts.

3.4 Information sources

Risk assessment will require information from varied sources and organization identifies such information through assumptions. Tier 1 will require information related to risk management structures and security related structures. Tier 2 will require information related to business processes, functions, system and enterprise architecture, external environments etc. Tier 3 will require information related to the design of technologies in use, environment in which the information systems operates usually, dependency on one system over the other, dependency of shared services etc.

3.5 Roles and Responsibilities

The following roles are typical in an organization but each organization is different so you may have some people who fill multiple roles or roles that are comprised by many people. The table below provides blanks for you to fill in the people who are responsible for each role.

Senior Management	
Risk Manager	
Technical Reviewer	
Network Administrator	
Department Heads	
Security Consultants	

4 Conducting the risk assessment

The second step in risk assessment is the actual phase during which the assessment is conducted and risks and threats are identified and ranked based on their severity. In order to accomplish this goal, I recommend that organization identify threat sources, threat events, vulnerabilities, impacts and the likelihood of risks. Even though information related to risks are gathered in the first step, some information are collected in this step as well. The main goal of this phase is to identify the complete risk scenarios that are likely to occur when vulnerabilities are exploited. The major sub tasks of conducting risk assessments include the following steps: identifying threat sources, identifying threat events, identifying vulnerabilities, determining the likelihood of threat occurrence, determining the impacts of threat on the organization processes, business functions, data etc., and determining the presence of risks on information security. The above order of tasks is not a standard one as organization reorder the steps based on their requirements. In some cases, certain steps will not be carried out at all. The most important activities in identifying threat sources will include identifying threat source inputs, the actual threat sources, determining the scope of threat sources and how they will impact the functioning of organization. The final sub task includes creation of new threat sources if needed. The next step in conducting risk assessments is to identify the various threat events and the sources that will cause the events to occur. Threat events occur based on threat sources as they form the catalyst for the event. It is the responsibility of organization to identify the threat events and the level of its impact. I recommend that threat events be categorized with various tiers of organization, ranging from tier 1 to tier 3.

4.1 Risk assessment scope

Generally, risk assessments are carried out at three levels of the organization. The tier 1 is organization level followed by mission and business process level and information systems level. The transparency of decisions taken on risks should be communicated to the whole team and organization wide awareness should be created as and when needed. There should also be possible communication between the various levels of the organization. Risk assessments help every level of operation in one way or the other and hence, the management should not hesitate in spending money for the procedures and techniques.

4.2 Risk Assessment Process

It is necessary to follow the process that is involved in risk assessment. It is necessary to follow the techniques in assessing risks, communicating the results to the team, monitoring the risk assessment process etc. There are four important steps in risk assessment process and they are preparing for the assessment, conducting the assessment, communicating the results of the assessment and maintaining and monitoring the assessment. Every step is composed of sub-tasks and the sub-tasks can be executed in ease with the help of supplemental guidance.

4.2.1 Collect information

In this stage, organization personnel will

Responsible person:	Risk manager and/or technical reviewer
Steps:	In general, the risk assessment will involve one or more of the following:
	• Visual inspection • Audit • Test • Interviews with designer, manufacturer, supplier, employees or other relevant parties.
	Some areas to include in this stage of the assessment include:
	Security Program Governance
	Executive Management has assigned roles and responsibilities for information security across its organization. This includes, but is not limited to, the following: documenting, disseminating, and periodically updating a formal information security program that addresses purpose, scope, roles, responsibilities, applicable laws and regulations, and the implementation of policies, standards, and procedures.
	Confidentiality Agreements
	Implement confidentiality or non-disclosure agreements with contractors and external entities to ensure the agency's needs for protection of classified information is met.
	Security Categorization
	Procedures to classify systems and information that is stored, processed, shared, or transmitted with respect to the type of data (e.g., confidential or sensitive) and its value to critical business functions are in place.
	Security Awareness
	Training is provided to all employees and contractors on an annual basis that addresses acceptable use and good computing practices for systems they are authorized to access. Content of training is based on the agency's policies addressing issues, such as, privacy requirements, virus protection, incident reporting, Internet use, notification to staff about monitoring activities, password requirements,

and consequences of legal and policy violations.

Human Resources Security

Policies and procedures that address purpose, scope, roles, responsibilities, and compliance to support personnel security requirements, such as access rights, disciplinary process, etc. are in place.

Position Categorization

Procedures for identifying system access needs by job function and screening criteria for individuals performing those functions are in place.

Personnel Separation

A process to terminate information system and physical access and ensure the return of all agency-related property (keys, id badges, etc.) when an individual changes assignments or separates from the agency is developed and implemented.

Third Party or Contractor Security

Personnel security requirements for third-party providers and procedures to monitor compliance are in place. Requirements are included in acquisition-related documents, such as service-level agreements, contracts, and memorandums of understanding.

Physical and Environmental Program

Policy and procedures that address the purpose, scope, roles, responsibilities, and compliance for physical and environmental security, such as security perimeter and entry controls, working in secure areas, equipment security, cabling security, fire detection and suppression, room temperature controls, etc. are in place.

Physical Access Monitoring

The need for monitored access to business areas is evaluated. In monitored areas, records for approved personnel access and sign-in sheets for visitors are maintained. Logs are periodically reviewed, violations or suspicious activities are investigated, and action is taken to address issues.

Physical Access Control

Physical access to facilities containing information systems is controlled and individual's authorization is verified before granting access.

Environmental Controls

The necessary environmental controls, based on a requirements assessment, which includes but is not limited to backup power to facilitate an orderly shutdown process, fire detection and suppression, temperature and humidity controls, water damage detection and mitigation are provisioned and properly maintained.

Secure Disposal of Equipment

Processes are in place to permanently remove any sensitive data and licensed software prior to disposal.

Disaster Recovery Planning

A Disaster Recovery Plan (DRP) is in place that supports the current business continuity needs of the agency.

Information Backup

Backup copies of information and software are completed on a routine schedule, tested regularly, and stored off-site.

Monitoring

System logging, and routine procedures to audit logs, security events, system use, systems alerts or failures, etc. are implemented and log information is in placed where it cannot be manipulated or altered.

Data Classification

Policies and processes to classify information in terms of its value, legal requirements, sensitivity, and criticality to organization are in place.

Access Controls

Policies and procedures are in place for appropriate levels of access to computer assets. Access controls include, but are not limited to:

- Password management, including the use of strong passwords, periodic password change, and restriction of sharing access and/or passwords. System access is authorized according to business need and password files are not stored in clear text or are otherwise adequately protected.
- Wireless access restrictions are in place, with organizational control over access points, prohibition and monitoring against rogue access points, appropriate configuration of wireless routers and

user devices, and policy, procedure, and training for technical staff and users are in place.

- Secure remote access procedures and policies are in place, and are known and followed by users.
- Mobile and portable systems and their data are protected through adequate security measures, such as encryption and secure passwords, and physical security, such as storing devices in a secure location and using cable locking devices.
- The tracking of access and authorities, including periodic audits of controls and privileges is in place.
- Networks challenge access requests (both user and system levels) and authenticate the requester prior to granting access.

Least Privilege

Configuration to the lowest privilege level necessary to execute legitimate and authorized business applications is implemented.

Data Storage and Portable Media Protection

Policies and procedures to protect data on electronic storage media, including CDs, USB drives, and tapes are in place. Procedures include labels on media to show sensitivity levels and handling requirements, rotation, retention and archival schedules, and appropriate destruction/disposal of media and data.

Malicious Code Protection

A regular patching process has been implemented to protect against malicious code. The process is automated when possible.

Intrusion Detection

Tools and techniques are utilized to monitor intrusion events, detect attacks, and provide identification of unauthorized system use.

Security Alerts and Advisories

The appropriate internal staff members receive security alerts/advisories on a regular basis and take appropriate actions in response to them.

Software and Information Integrity

Information systems/applications detect and protect against unauthorized changes to software and information.

Information Input Accuracy, Completeness, and Validity

Information systems/applications check data inputs for accuracy, completeness, and validity.

Device Hardening

Operating system and application level updates, patches, and hot fixes are applied as soon as they become available and are fully tested. Services on the computing devices are only enabled where there is a demonstrated business need and only after a risk assessment.

Lock-Out for Inactive Computing Devices

The automatic locking of the computing device after a period of inactivity is enforced.

Data Storage

Data that needs additional protection is stored on pre-defined servers, rather than on computing devices, for both data protection and backup/recovery reasons. Confidential, sensitive, and/or personal (notice-triggering) information is not stored on computing devices without a careful risk assessment and adequate security measures.

Network Protection

Network and communication protection policies and procedures are in place. These documents outline the procedures to authorize all connections to network services. Authorization is based on an evaluation of sensitive or critical business applications, classification of data stored on the system, and physical location of the system (e.g., public area, private access, secure access, etc.).

Transmission Integrity and Confidentiality

Data is protected from unauthorized disclosure during transmission. Data classification is used to determine what security measures to employ, including encryption or physical measures.

Boundary Protection

Equipment designed for public access (i.e. Web servers dispensing public information) is protected. These are segregated from the internal networks that control them. Access into internal networks by authorized staff is controlled to prevent unauthorized entry.

Protect and Secure Network Infrastructure

Policies and procedures for technology upgrades, network

	equipment (e.g., servers, routers, firewalls, and switches), patches and upgrades, firewall and server configurations, and server hardening, etc. are in place.
	Incident Reporting
	Proper incident reporting policies and procedures are in place. These include training employees and contractors to identify and report incidents, the reporting of incidents immediately upon discovery, and preparation and submission of follow-up written reports.
Duration	2-4 weeks

4.2.2 Identify systems or processes at risk

In this stage, organization personnel will Identify potential dangers to information and system (threats) and system weakness that could be exploited (vulnerabilities) associated to generate the threat / vulnerability pair. Identifying vulnerabilities increases the likelihood of detecting risks and threats. Since there are various business processes, functions and information systems, it is necessary to understand the vulnerabilities based on the threat events and threat sources. The most critical vulnerabilities are those that are found in tier 1 as they cause adverse effects to the entire organization when exploited by threat sources. This is because threats at organizational tier will cause disruption of business processes and functions at all levels. Vulnerabilities that are exploited at tier 2 will span across the business processes and functions only, and it may not cause complete organizational impacts. Vulnerabilities at tier 3 cause problems in information technology systems and the environments in which they operate in. Threat sources and vulnerabilities also have many to many relationships as one threat source causes multiple vulnerabilities and one vulnerability is exploited by multiple threat sources and events. Once a vulnerability is identified, a rough estimate of its severity is calculated. Later, when the impact of the vulnerability is identified along with other assumptions and predisposing conditions, the actual vulnerability is assessed and documented.

When vulnerabilities are assessed and documented, all granular details should be recorded. Vulnerabilities have been found in all levels of organization. Due to the increase in the size of organization, the business processes and functions have increased as well. This has also increased the number of information systems that are used for performing the business functions. As a result, the number of vulnerabilities is on the rise and organizations face complexity in identifying all these vulnerabilities. Thus, organizations should effectively use the vulnerability assessment task to identify and catalogue vulnerabilities based on impact and the threat sources that exploit them. Also, the predisposing conditions within organization are analyzed and vulnerabilities corresponding to those conditions are catalogued as well.

Responsible person:	Risk manager and/or technical reviewer
Steps:	1. Consider the system's connections, dependencies with other systems, inherited risks and controls, risks from software faults and staff errors and malicious intent, and such factors as proximity to the Internet, incorrect file permissions, risks from maintenance procedures and personnel changes. 2. Describe how each vulnerability creates a risk to the system in terms of confidentiality, integrity, availability, auditability or accountability elements that may result in a compromise of the system.
Duration	1-6 months

4.2.3 Evaluate the likelihood of harm occurring

In this stage, organization personnel will determine the likelihood of occurrence for a threat exploiting a related vulnerability given the existing controls. The likelihood is determined based on various factors ranging from the characteristics of threat sources and the threat events, assumptions, vulnerabilities and predisposing conditions and the techniques employed by organizations to overcome the threats. As discussed above, the likelihood of threat event is determined using a three step process. Organizations will assess the likelihood of threats when the threat events will be initiated followed by assessing likelihood when the threat events are actually initiated. For adversarial threat events, the characteristics of threat sources are used for determining the likelihood and for nonadversarial threat events, the severity and duration of the threat event is used. When a threat event is found to have no predisposing condition or vulnerability, the likelihood of the threat is considered very low. Determining the likelihood of threat depends on factors such as organizational approach towards risk and risk tolerance, weighing risk factors and treating unknown risk factors. There are various algorithms for weighing risk factors and some of them are using the maximum value of a couple of likelihoods, the minimum value of likelihoods or taking the average of the likelihood values.

Responsible person:	Risk manager	
Steps:	For each risk, determine the likelihood. Likelihood of occurrence is based on a number of factors that include system architecture, system environment, information system access and existing controls; the presence, motivation, tenacity, strength and nature of the threat; the presence of vulnerabilities; and the effectiveness of existing controls.	
	Likelihood	**Description**
	Negligible	Unlikely ever to occur
	Very Low	Likely to occur two/three times every five years
	Low	Likely to occur once every year or less
	Medium	Likely to occur once every six months or less
	High	Likely to occur once per month or less
	Very High	Likely to occur multiple times per month
	Extreme	Likely to occur multiple times per day
Duration:	2-4 weeks	

4.2.4 Evaluate the impact

In this stage, organization personnel will determine the severity of impact on the system by an exploited vulnerability. The impact of threat events of organization is also determined based on factors such as, organization's measures for tackling threat, characteristics of threat events and sources and the identification of vulnerabilities. The impact of threats on organization functioning determines the severity. Also, the possibility of one threat initiating other threat events determines the severity. The severity of threat events is also determined by analyzing the condition of various assets in organization and the targets of threat sources. The impact of threat events at tier 1 and tier 2 are communicated to resources at tier 3. Based on the impact of threat events and the likelihood of threats, the risks are determined. The calculation of risk determines the extent to which organizations are affected. Sometimes, organizations take much uncertainty into the determination of risk. All uncertainty should be communicated to all the levels of organization. Based on the risk assessment, organizations will list the threats and prioritize the same.

Responsible person:	Risk manager
Steps:	1. Brainstorm ideas and group under appropriate risk headings. Consider the effects on people (staff, students and other people), information, physical assets and finances, reputation to determine the magnitude or severity of impact on the system's operational capabilities and the information it handles, if the threat is realized and exploits the associated vulnerability. Determine the severity of impact for each threat / vulnerability pair by evaluating the potential loss in each security category (confidentiality, integrity, availability, auditability, accountability) based on the system's information security level. 2. Research incidents where this occurred and identify the impact to the business. Revise impact figures to reflect differences between organization and the benchmark incident company. Rank the impact using the following labels.

Label	Description
Insignificant	Little or no impact
Minor	Minimal effort to repair, restore or reconfigure
Significant	Small but tangible harm, maybe noticeable by a limited audience, some embarrassment, some effort to repair
Damaging	Damage to reputation, loss of confidence, significant effort to repair
Serious	Considerable system outage, loss of connected customers, business confidence, compromise of large amount information

	Critical	Extended outage, permanent loss of resource, triggering business continuity procedures, complete compromise of information
Duration:	1-4 weeks	

4.2.5 Determine risk for the item

In this stage, organization personnel will determine the risk for respective item:

Responsible person:	Risk manager
Steps:	Plot the previously determined impact and likelihood values to determine the risk.

Likelihood	Impact Severity					
	Insignificant	Minor	Significant	Damaging	Serious	Critical
Negligible	Low	Low	Low	Low	Low	Low
Very Low	Low	Low	Low	Low	Moderate	Moderate
Low	Low	Low	Moderate	Moderate	High	High
Medium	Low	Low	Moderate	High	High	High
High	Low	Moderate	High	High	High	High
Very High	Low	Moderate	High	High	High	High
Extreme	Low	Moderate	High	High	High	High

Duration:	1 week

Once the risks and corresponding impact is assessed, the priority of the items can be determined using a four-quadrant graph (an example of which is provided below):

Risk Management - Prioritized Action Items

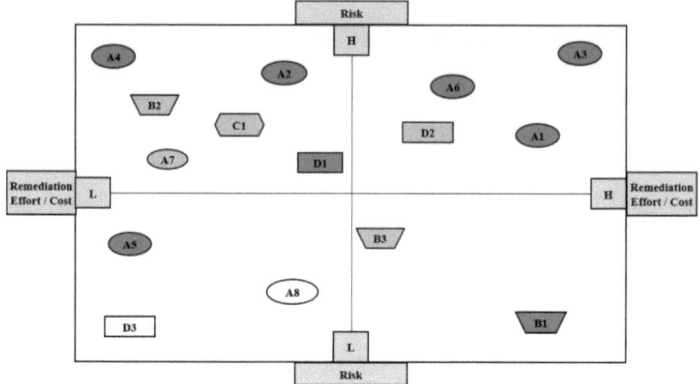

4.2.6 Investigate options for eliminating or controlling risks

In this stage, organization personnel will investigate viable options for mitigating or eliminating assessed risks:

Responsible person:	Risk manager, system administrator, or technical reviewer
Steps:	• Recommend controls and safeguards if the risk level is moderate or high. • Determine residual (remaining) likelihood of occurrence if controls and safeguards are implemented • Determine residual severity of impact if candidate controls and safeguards are implemented • Determine residual risk levels Assign a work effort and benefit to each item. **Work Effort** High -- Requires significantly more resource, time and budget Moderate -- Requires average resource, time and budget Low -- Requires very little resource, time and budget **Benefit** High -- Significantly reduce risk to an acceptable level Moderate -- May reduce risk to an acceptable level Low-- Does not reduce risk to an acceptable level
Duration:	2-4 weeks

4.2.7

4.2.8 Prioritize action and decide on control measures

In this stage, organization personnel will prioritize actions and decide on mitigation measures:

Responsible person:	Senior management
Steps:	Each risk identified should be prioritized. Organizations can use a high, medium or low ranking system or one that has more levels if desired. **High risk:** Situation critical, stop work immediately or consider cessation of work process. Directly leads to the disclosure of private and sensitive information, or compromise of the underlying target environment, or direct negative financial or business reputation impact. Must be fixed today, consider short and/or long term actions. Time frame: Immediately **Medium risk:** It is very important. Potential for compromise of private and sensitive data, or indirect negative financial or business reputation impact, or compromise of a small number of application account credentials. Must be fixed this week, consider short and/or long term actions. Time frame: This week **Low risk:** It is still important, but can be dealt with through scheduled maintenance or similar type programming. Does not directly or indirectly impact their financial or business reputation, or minimal information disclosure, or compromise of a single non-administrative account, limited liability problems which are considered low business risk. However, if solution is quick and easy, then fix it today. Review and/or manage by routine procedures. Time frame: 1-3 months
Duration:	1-2 weeks

4.2.9 Implement controls

In this stage, organization personnel will implement controls related to mitigation measures:

Responsible person:	IT director for technology controls, HR director for HR procedures, departmental management for processes or procedures to be implemented in that department.
Steps:	Actual implementation steps will depend upon the controls selected.
Duration:	TBD

4.2.10 Measure the effectiveness of implemented actions

In this stage, organization personnel will measure the effectiveness of implemented actions or measures to mitigate assessment risks:

Responsible person:	Auditor
Steps:	Establish metrics to evaluate the effectiveness and document the actual and expected values.
Duration:	2-4 weeks

4.3 Assessing risks at organizational level

The risk assessment conducted at tier 1, organizational level focuses on the policies and strategies followed by organization. Some of the common risks that are assessed at organizational level include the types of threats that are focused on the particular organization, weaknesses identified on the information systems of organization, the likelihood of threat when the information related to organization is lost, risks of new technologies being used at organizational level etc. The risk assessment conducted at tier 1 is mostly based on assumptions and are not realistic. A risk assessment is considered as proper one when the results of the assessments made at tier 2 are taken as inputs for risk assessment practices on tier 1. This type of assessment is best suited when organization follows the same principles of the parent companies and when the mission of organization is the same as the mission of the business process. When the above two criteria are not met, the results of tier 2 assessment cannot be directly used as inputs for tier 1. Expert analysis should be carried out before setting out the requirements. When the risk assessment phase is completed at organizational level, the results should be shared with organization entities present in the two lower tiers.

4.4 Assessing risks at the business process level

The risk assessment at tier 2 should focus mainly on the protection of business processes and functions. It should also focus on the importance of information security systems along with the information on when and where such systems should be used. The risk assessment at level 2 should also focus on the business continuity plan of organization. The other important consideration for assessing risks at business process level is the degree of security provided by the information security architecture. Similar to tier 1, the results of risk assessment on tier 2 is shared with organizational entities of tier 3. Also, as said above, the results of tier 2 risk assessment are sometimes carried forward as inputs to tier 1. In such cases, the results are shared not only with organizational entities of tier 3 but also to tier 1.

4.5 Assessing risks at the information system tier

The requirements of risk assessment for information system tier are based on the results of tier 2 risk assessments and the software development life cycle. As compared to the processes of software development life cycle, the risk assessment should also be carried out in the initiation phase itself. When the risk assessments are carried out at the initiation phase, the risks and threats that will cause serious damage to the confidentiality, integrity and reliability of organization data can be identified. This will enable product managers to decide on the level of security needed for organization and the business process. When the risk assessments are completed at initiation phase, they are carried forward to the next levels, thereby updating the document based on the results. The risk assessment at information system tier will include information about possible vulnerabilities along with the risks that will be caused by such vulnerabilities. It should also provide information on how to overcome such risks and threats. The results obtained by the risk assessment of tier 3 are shared with both the higher levels of organization – organization level and business process level.

Risk assessments are often coupled together with the various steps in risk management framework. Some of the common steps include categorizing the risks followed by selection of security controls for the prevention of risks. Even though most of the steps are carried out at tier 3, some steps are still performed at tier 1 and tier 2. The various steps in risk management framework will help identify the security awareness of organization and the use of security related functions. The first step in RMF is categorization of security related concepts. The risk assessment will help in identifying various threat sources, threat events, vulnerabilities etc. which will then help organization to enable possible security information systems. The second step in risk management framework is the selection of various security related controls and information systems. Once the security guidelines are in place, the risk assessment will ensure that the organization will modify the security controls based on information obtained from business processes. Also, the threat information should be used to update the security controls. When the security control is in place, it will be checked for vulnerability and the possibility of occurrence of single point of failure and if such vulnerability exists, it will be termed as risk. The threat information should be updated as and when needed so as to enhance the security controls in place.

The third and important step in risk assessment is the implementation of various security controls that are selected in step 2. When the controls are implemented, they are checked for the presence of vulnerability and based on the results; the supplementary controls are installed as well. Some of the information security related products are more prone to certain types of threat sources, thereby requiring frequent updates of risk assessment and risk analysis. The risk assessment will help organization analyze the cost involved in providing security to the threat information and vulnerabilities. Whenever new threat events and threat sources are identified, organizational level risk assessment should be carried out so as to stay on top of the requirements. The fourth step is the use of security related assessments to update risk assessments. This will ensure organization identify critical vulnerabilities in the environment and the severity of those vulnerabilities. When the threat related information is gathered, they are shared with the officials on board, and authorizations are provided for them to carry out security related techniques. Another important step in the risk assessment analysis is the monitoring of information systems on an ongoing basis. Continuous monitoring ensures that the security controls are updated based on latest threat information and the latest security standards are incorporated in the system. The result of this six step process is then used for defining risk management strategy.

4.6 Communicating risk information

The information gathered by risk assessment and risk analysis should be shared with the entities of organization. The major benefits of communicating risk information include raising awareness among the employees on the various inputs and outputs of risk assessment, using intermediate results as input for further studies etc. Consistency should be maintained in sharing the results and separate standards should be in force, for the transmission of results. Organizations should set policies and framework for communication of risk assessments.

A Risk Assessment report applies to a selected information system. An information system is a group of computing and network components that share a business function, under common ownership and management. The Report should include:

- A documented system inventory, listing all system components and establishing the system boundary for the purposes of the Report

- Documentation of the system's policies and procedures, and details of its operation

- List of threat / vulnerability pairs, with severity of impact and likelihood of occurrence

- List of safeguards for controlling these threats and vulnerabilities

- List of recommended changes, with approximate levels of effort for each

- For each recommended change, the resulting reduction in risk

- The level of residual risk that will remain after the recommended changes are implemented